MW01230052

HOW WIDE ARE
HEAVEN'S DOORS?
The Biblical Case for Ultimate Restoration

By George W. Sarris

PUBLISHING Grace Will Succeed

GWS PUBLISHING Grace Will Succeed

Excepts and comments in this book are taken directly from,
Heaven's Doors . . . Wider Than You Ever Believed! which
was awarded the Silver Medal in Theology in the 2018
Illumination Book Awards for exemplary Christian literature.
That book is available as a paperback, eBook or as an
audiobook on Amazon.com.

Unless otherwise noted, Scripture quotations are taken from
The Holy Bible, New International Version (1984 Edition)
copyright © 1973, 1978, 1984 by Biblica, Inc. Used by
permission.

ISBN 978-0-9800853-5-8 (Paperback Edition)

Library of Congress Control Number: 2020925103

Editor, Jack Linn
Cover design by Fred Duanno & Debbi Stocco

Introduction

Saint Anselm defined God as *"that Being than which none greater can be conceived."*

I think that's a pretty good definition, and as I think about it . . .

I can conceive of a God who is all-powerful, all-wise and good.

I can conceive of a God whose power is irresistible, whose love is unconditional and who never gives up on any of those He created in His image.

I can conceive of a God before whom *every* knee will one day freely and joyfully bow, and *every* tongue will one day freely and joyfully confess that Jesus Christ is Lord to the glory of God the Father.

I can conceive of a God who will one day restore

all of His creation to the perfection He intended, so that at the end of time He will once again look out on all that He has made and declare that it is *very good!*

One of the most common responses I receive from those who hear that I believe in this ultimate restoration of all things is, *"I sure wish that were true, but . . ."* and then they quickly bring up the subject of hell.

Although they would never admit it, what they are actually saying is,

> "Deep down inside, I wish God were different. I wish He were more loving, or wiser, or more powerful than He is."

Although they would never admit it, what they are actually saying is,

> "I can conceive of a God who is greater than the one I worship. One who would be able to save *everyone* He created. But I am forced to believe in this lesser God because of what I've been told the Bible teaches about hell."

My purpose for writing this short book is to briefly introduce you to some of the teachings from Church history and Scripture that have been misunderstood, misinterpreted and misrepresented to show that what most people have been told about the nature and duration of hell is *not* true.

My purpose for writing this short book is to show that the God of the Bible is truly *that Being than which none greater can be conceived!*

What Is Hell?

A good place to begin is by asking the question, *"What is hell?"*

That word has been defined in different ways down through the centuries, from a place of literal fire . . . to a kingdom of darkness ruled by the devil and his demons . . . to what is the most common definition today as separation from God. But for most people holding to the traditional view of hell, two components are essential.

First, hell is a place or condition of *conscious misery*.

And second, that misery will *never, ever, ever, ever, ever end*.

I say that somewhat dramatically because, in my experience, most Christians today have never really thought through the implications of what they say they believe. Punishment for sin is not the issue. We see sin punished all the time in this life, and God has made it clear that there is punishment in the age or ages to come.

But punishment that *never* ends is a completely different matter. It brings to mind cruel tyrants who torture subjects who don't do their bidding. Endless, conscious misery is the most horrific thing you could possibly imagine. And if you really believed it was true, you would be weeping almost every moment of every day over the fate of those who are lost – especially those you know and love personally.

However, that understanding of hell was *not* the teaching of the Early Christian Church. It is *not* the teaching of the Bible. And it is *contrary* to what is revealed in Scripture about the nature and character of God.

The Teaching of the
Early Christian Church

What the Early Church believed and taught is important because the early Christians were closest to Jesus and the Apostles. They read the New Testament in their native tongue. They had the greatest impact on the surrounding culture of any time in history. And they established the Faith that we now profess.

They were the ones who wrote the Apostles Creed and the Nicene Creed to explain clearly what true Christians believed. They were the ones who formulated the doctrines of the Divinity of Christ and the Trinity. And they were the ones who assembled the 27 books we now call the New Testament.

During the first 500 years after Christ, a prominent view, and according to some scholars, the dominant view within the leadership and laity of the Church was that God will ultimately restore *all* of His creation to the perfection He initially intended.

Clement of Alexandria

For example, that was the view of Clement of Alexandria. Clement was born around AD 150, within a couple of generations of Jesus and the apostles. For him, to believe that God is *powerless* to save all was unthinkable, because that would mean God is weak. To believe that God *does not want* to save all was also unthinkable, because that would mean that God is not good. For Clement, God's ultimate plan is the salvation of the universe.

> "For either the Lord does not care for all men; and this is the case either because He is unable, which is not to be thought for it would be a proof of weakness, or because He is unwilling, which is not the attribute of a good being . . . Or He does care for all, which is befitting for Him who has become Lord of all. He is Savior; not of some, and of others not ... For all things are arranged with a view

8

to the salvation of the universe by the Lord of the universe . . ."[1]

In response to those who thought that God takes vengeance on the wicked, Clement said, *"No."* That could not be the case because that would be returning evil for evil. Clement saw God as One who always acts for the good of those He created.

> "But as children are chastised by their teacher, or their father, so are we by Providence. But God does not punish, for punishment is retaliation for evil. He chastises, however, for good to those who are chastised, collectively and individually."[2]

Gregory of Nyssa

Another leader in the Early Church who believed in the ultimate restoration of all was Gregory of Nyssa. Gregory added the phrase, *"I believe in the life of the world to come,"* to the Nicene Creed. He died around AD 395 and is still revered as one of the greatest of the Eastern Church fathers. In AD 787, the Seventh General Council of the Church honored Gregory by naming him, *Father of the Fathers*.

Does God punish forever with terrifying pain?

Gregory explained that those who are immature think this and fear it. They are thus motivated to flee from wickedness. However, those with more maturity understand the true purpose of after-death punishment. It's a remedial process instituted by God to ultimately restore to health those who are sick. Like a skilled surgeon who doesn't stop until his work is finished, God does not give up on those He created.

> "If, however, the soul remains unhealed, the remedy is dispensed in the life that follows this . . . and this to the thoughtless sort is held out as the threat of a terrible correction, in order that through fear of this painful retribution they may gain the wisdom of fleeing from wickedness: while by those of more intelligence it is believed to be a remedial process ordered by God to bring back man, His peculiar creature, to the grace of his primal condition."[3]

Gregory explained,

> "In due course evil will pass over into non-existence; it will disappear utterly from the realm of existence. Divine and

uncompounded goodness will encompass within itself every rational nature; no single being created by God will fail to achieve the kingdom of God." [4]

Other well-known leaders within the Early Church who believed in the ultimate restoration of all, include Origen, Didymus, St. Anthony, St. Pamphilus Martyr, Methodius, St. Macrina, St. Evagrius Ponticus, Diodore of Tarsus, Theodore of Mopsuestia, St. John of Jerusalem, Rufinus, Cassian, St. Isaac of Nineveh, St. John of Dalyatha, Ps. Dionysius the Areopagite, St. Maximus the Confessor, and John the Scot Eriugena. [5]

Even St. Augustine, the most influential supporter of endless punishment in the Early Church, acknowledged that in his day

> ". . . some – indeed very many – deplore the notion of the eternal punishment of the damned and their interminable and perpetual misery." [6]

How Wide Are Heaven's Doors?

The Teaching of the Bible:
Divine Judgment

Conscious suffering that never ends was not the teaching of the Early Church, and it is also not the teaching of Scripture, although most people today think it is.

How Long is *Forever?*

The passage most often pointed to as the clearest statement in the entire Bible that punishment in hell is endless, is Matthew 25:46. In that verse, Jesus says that the wicked "will go away to *eternal* punishment, but the righteous to *eternal* life."

That seems pretty clear – the punishment referred to is *eternal*, so it must be endless, right? Well, actually, no!

The first thing to point out in this passage is that the Greek word, *aion*, here translated "eternal" or "everlasting" or "forever" depending on which version of the Bible you are reading, does not mean never-ending. It actually means the *end is not known*. It refers to

> "a period of time – longer or shorter, past or future – the boundaries of which are concealed, obscure, unseen or unknown."[7]

It's a word that you might use if you were standing on a beach looking out toward the horizon. From that perspective, it seems like the ocean goes on forever. But, of course, it doesn't. There is a shoreline out there somewhere. It's just that when you're standing on a beach looking out, you don't know where that shoreline is. From that standpoint, the place where the ocean ends is unknown.

That word is used in numerous places in the Septuagint – the ancient Greek translation of the Old Testament that Jesus and the Apostles quoted from – where it regularly refers to things that have or will come to an end.

For example, after Jonah ran away from God and was swallowed by the great fish, he had a change of heart and decided to pray. In his prayer he tells

14

how long he expected to be imprisoned.

> "To the roots of the mountains I sank
> down; the earth beneath barred me in
> *forever.*"[8]

Jonah didn't know how long his situation would last. In this case, *forever* turned out to be three days, and was followed by his release.

In many places in the Old Testament, the sacrifices and offerings made by the priests were said to be established by God "forever" – they were "eternal" statutes. But those statutes didn't last forever, and they were never intended to last forever.

The sacrificial system lasted for a very long time, almost 1,000 years. But it eventually came to an end. The first Temple was destroyed by the Babylonians in 587/86 BC, and the rebuilt Temple was destroyed by Roman forces in AD 70.

There's no longer a Jewish priesthood. There's no longer a Temple in Jerusalem. There's no longer a system of sacrifices being offered. The purpose for that system was fulfilled, and it was no longer needed. It's now been superseded by the New Covenant in Christ.

A second argument made by those who believe that Matthew 25:46 teaches endless punishment was first suggested by St. Augustine – who, by the way, did *not* read Greek. He said,

> "For Christ, in the very same passage, included both punishment and life in one and the same sentence . . . If both are 'eternal,' it follows necessarily that either both are to be taken as long-lasting but finite, or both as endless and perpetual." [9]

Is that true? If an adjective is used twice in the same sentence, must it necessarily mean the same thing each time? Again, the answer is no.

For example, if Goliath had fought David in front of Mt. Everest, a person could honestly say, "A *tall* man is standing in front of a *tall* mountain." But no one would think the man and the mountain were the same size. The adjective *tall* derives its meaning from what it refers to – in the first instance to a man and in the second to a mountain.

In Matthew 25:46, the adjective Jesus used refers to two completely different things – life and punishment. Eternal life is *divine life* that comes from God. That divine life never ends. Eternal

16

punishment is *divine punishment* from His hand. The duration of that divine punishment may certainly be temporary, lasting as long as necessary until it accomplishes its purpose.

Third, if we take the time to look at the context of what Jesus is actually talking about in Matthew 25:46, we'll make an amazing discovery. Jesus' statement occurs at the end of a discourse that He gives privately to His disciples, extending from Matthew 24:4 to the verse we're looking at – 25:46. The question that prompts the entire talk is

> ". . . what will be the sign of your coming and of the *end* of the *aion*?"[10]

Aion is the same word that's translated *eternal* in the verse we've been discussing. The Greek word *aion* in Matthew 25:46 *cannot* mean endless because the *aion* in question is said to have an end!

The Rich Man and Lazarus

Another of the passages most often said to support the idea that the Bible teaches endless punishment is the parable of the Rich Man and Lazarus in Luke 16.

Most Bible versions say that the rich man is in

hell. He's described as being "in torment and agony in this fire." A great chasm has been fixed between the rich man and Lazarus, and those who want to cross over that chasm cannot. That sounds pretty convincing!

However, if we take a closer look at the passage, a few things bring that interpretation into question.

First of all, the rich man was *not* in hell. He was in *Hades,* and Revelation 20:13 specifically says that *Hades* will one day *give up* the dead who are in it.

Second, this is a parable – a fictional story designed to teach a spiritual truth. What Jesus did was similar to what a modern speaker would do when making reference to a book like *The Lion, the Witch and the Wardrobe* by C.S. Lewis. He could clearly point out some very important truths about life in this world, without putting his stamp of approval on the existence of talking animals in another world.

The audience for this parable was made up of tax collectors and sinners who were spiritually poor and recognized their need for God. And Pharisees and teachers of the law who were materially rich and had deceived themselves into thinking they were favored by God. Like the rich man in the parable, many of those religious leaders were actually clothed in purple and fine linen and lived in luxury every day.

The point of the parable was that those rich religious leaders wouldn't repent even if one were to rise from the dead.

Third, the parable was told *before* the crucifixion and resurrection of Christ. Neither Abraham, nor the rich man, nor Lazarus could do anything to make it possible to go from one side of the chasm to the other. That was the purpose of Jesus' death and resurrection. Christ bridged the chasm.

Gehenna

It's often said that Jesus spoke of hell more often than any of the other New Testament writers. That claim is actually true. But it's also *not* true.

The claim is based on the number of times Jesus used the Greek word *Gehenna,* the term most commonly translated as *hell* in modern versions of the Bible. *Gehenna* is used 12 times in the New Testament, and 11 of those times it's used by Jesus Himself. The other use is in the book of James.

So if we're looking at how many times Jesus used the word that's translated *hell* in Bible translations, compared to how many times others in the New Testament used that same word, we'd be correct in saying that Jesus spoke of *hell* more often than anyone else.

However, the real issue is not how many times Jesus used a particular word. The real issue is what Jesus meant when He used it, and what His listeners understood when they heard it.

What comes to your mind when you hear the word *Auschwitz?* In the future, it's possible that the word will take on a more metaphorical meaning. But right now, while the actual place still exists as a museum and in the memories of some who knew it firsthand, it reminds us of the repulsion, shame and horrible deaths experienced by those who suffered in Nazi concentration camps in World War II.

Like Auschwitz in our day, the *Gehenna* that Jesus spoke of was an actual place that people could visit. It had been associated with child sacrifice in the past and was then most likely used as the common dump of the city. The corpses of the worst criminals were flung into it unburied.

20

Its stench was stifling. Fires were lit to purify the contaminated air. And it spoke to Jesus and His listeners of repulsion, shame and horrible death.

Instead of experiencing honor like their ancestors whose bodies were treated reverently when they died, those cast into *Gehenna* would experience the immense dishonor associated with those whose bodies had been disposed of in a dump to become an object of scorn for the masses. In an honor/shame culture like that in the ancient Near East, that was a fate worse than death.

Solomon expressed very well the thought that would be in the minds of the 1st century Jewish leaders who listened to Jesus.

> "A man may have a hundred children and live many years; yet no matter how long he lives, if he cannot enjoy his prosperity and does not receive proper burial, I say that a stillborn child is better off than he." [11]

Gehenna was definitely a reference to God's judgment. But it was a judgment on earth.

The Unpardonable Sin

One of the greatest fears that Christians have had

down through the centuries is that they've somehow committed the *unpardonable* sin – a sin so serious that the person who commits it can never be forgiven, and must spend eternity in conscious torment in hell.

The fear is based on a comment Jesus made when He healed a demon-possessed man. Instead of seeing what Jesus did as a true miracle of God, some of the religious leaders accused Him of being possessed by the devil, having an unclean spirit, and driving out demons by using the power of the devil himself.

Mark records Jesus' response with these words,

> "I tell you the truth, all the sins and blasphemies of men will be forgiven them. But whoever blasphemes against the Holy Spirit will never be forgiven; he is guilty of an eternal sin." [12]

Those are strong words, for sure. And they definitely give the impression that this is a very serious sin!

However, if we look carefully at what Jesus is saying, the first thing to note is that, except for the sin against the Holy Spirit, Jesus says that *all* sins and blasphemies of men will be forgiven them.

This clearly implies a great hope for the possibility of an ultimate restoration for all those who do not accuse Jesus of being possessed by the devil, having an unclean spirit, and accomplishing His miracles by the devil's power.

The second thing we should be aware of is that the word *never* in this passage is not in the Greek text. Jesus did *not* say the person will *never* be forgiven. He actually said that whoever blasphemes against the Holy Spirit will not be forgiven "either in this age or in the age to come," as it reads in Matthew. [13]

Blasphemy against the Holy Spirit is attributing God's work to Satan. It's saying *no* to God. Obviously, as long as that continues, nothing can be done. It's impossible for someone to experience God's forgiving grace when that person won't accept it, whether that occurs in this age, the age to come, or in one of the ages to come.

However, if hell is a place designed to bring people to a place where they recognize their need for God's saving grace in Christ, when they *stop* resisting and truly repent, then God's forgiveness is granted and heaven's doors are opened.

The Narrow Door

Jesus was once asked a very direct question about who would be saved.

> "Lord, are only a few people going to be saved?"[14]

He answered the question with a parable to encourage His listeners to make every effort to enter through the *narrow door*. Once the door is closed, many will try to enter but will be unable. They will knock and plead, but won't be let in. The result will be "weeping and gnashing of teeth" when they see Abraham, Isaac, Jacob and all the prophets sitting at a feast in the kingdom of God, but they themselves are thrown out.

Unfortunately, the question phrased in most English translations gives a completely different sense from the question that was actually asked. The wording in the original Greek is,

> "Lord, are they few in number, those *who are being saved*?"

It wasn't a question about how many people would *ultimately* be saved. It was a question about the number of people *at that time* who were accepting the message that Jesus brought. The kingdom of God is not only a future reality. It's a kingdom that Jesus began to establish while He was here on earth.

In a similar passage in the Sermon on the Mount, Jesus encouraged those in His audience to

> "Enter through the narrow gate. For wide is the gate and broad is the road that leads to destruction, and many enter through it. But small is the gate and narrow the road that leads to life, and only a few find it." [15]

As with many places where Jesus talks about life, He was not addressing the *afterlife* in this passage. Jesus was talking about pursuing a truly meaningful and productive life in the here and now. That life is actually found by comparatively few people. By contrast, there are many unproductive avenues in life that are broad, easy to follow and well traveled.

You simply need to look around at all the trivial things people pursue – the biggest house, newest car, whitest teeth, most Facebook friends, latest iPhone – to see the truth of that statement.

Repentance is impossible

The book of Hebrews presents some very sobering words about those who have fallen away from the faith.

> "It is impossible for those who have once been enlightened, who have tasted the heavenly gift, who have shared in the Holy Spirit, who have tasted the goodness of the word of God and the powers of the coming age, if they fall away, to be brought back to repentance, because to their loss they are crucifying the son of God all over again and subjecting him to public disgrace." [16]

If it's *impossible* for someone who's fallen away to be brought back to repentance, are we not forced to conclude that they can never ultimately be restored? No.

The word *impossible* here has a force similar to what Jesus said to His disciples after He told them it would be easier for a camel to go through the eye of a needle than for a rich man to enter the kingdom of God.

In response to their question, *"Who then can be*

saved?" Jesus said,

> "With man this is impossible, but with God *all things are possible*." [17]

The writer of Hebrews is saying that it's impossible for *people* to bring back someone who has fallen away and thus subjected Jesus to public disgrace. But it's not impossible for *God* to restore that individual.

These words in Hebrews would seem to apply to the apostle Peter, and it certainly may have been on Peter's mind after he denied Christ three times.

He had "once been enlightened . . . tasted the heavenly gift . . . shared in the Holy Spirit . . . tasted the goodness of the word of God and the powers of the coming age," and he had "fallen away and subjected Jesus to public disgrace."

The other disciples tried to restore Peter with their words. However, it was not until Jesus Himself came and spoke directly to Peter, asking him three times if he loved Him, that Peter was restored.

The Lake of Fire

The last judgment passage we'll look at relates directly to the fate of the wicked after they die.

27

The wicked will be cast into the Lake of Fire. We're told,

> "the cowardly, the unbelieving, the vile, the murderers, the sexually immoral, those who practice magic arts, the idolaters and all liars – their place will be in the fiery lake of burning sulfur. This is the second death." [18]

We're also informed,

> "the devil who had deceived them was thrown into the lake of fire and sulfur where the beast and the false prophet were, and they will be tormented day and night forever and ever." [19]

That definitely sounds like something horrendous beyond description. But the words in their original language give a much different picture of what the purpose of the Lake of Fire is than what is normally thought.

The word translated *sulfur* originally referred to fire from heaven. It's connected with sulfur because it was used in pagan religious rites for *purification*.

Pre-Roman civilizations used it as a medicine, a fumigant, a bleaching agent and in incense. And the Romans used sulfur or fumes from its combustion as an insecticide, and to purify a sick room to cleanse its air of evil.

The term translated *torment* originally referred to the action of an inspector who sought to test the quality of something, as with good vs. forged money. In its proper sense, it is a means of testing and proving.

For the apostle John who authored the book of Revelation, and for his readers in the ancient world, the Lake of Fire was a refiner's fire, *not* a place of unending torture with no purpose other than to inflict pain. Its purpose was to purify and cleanse from evil in the age to come.

God is good. And all His punishments have a good purpose.

The Teaching of the Bible: Divine Hope

Now that we've looked at some of the judgment passages of Scripture and seen that they do *not* teach endless punishment, it's time to look at passages in the Bible that give hope that one day all of those God created in His image will experience the peace and joy of being in His presence.

Who Is Jesus Christ?

The best place for us to begin is by looking at who the Bible says Jesus Christ is, and why He came.

The angel who appeared to the shepherds on that glorious night to announce the birth of the promised Messiah did *not* say, "I bring you good news of great joy that will be for *some* of the people." He did not even say, "I bring you good news of great joy that will be for *most* of the people." The angel said,

"I bring you good news of great joy that will be for *all the people*. Today in the town of David, a *Savior* has been born to you; He is Christ, the Lord" [20]

That message was made clear by John the Baptist when he revealed who Jesus was.

"Behold, the Lamb of God *who takes away the sin of the world*." [21]

The people in the Samaritan town of Sychar, after spending two days with Jesus, said to the woman,

"We no longer believe just because of what you said; now we have heard for ourselves, and we know that this man really is the *Savior of the world*." [22]

The apostle John acknowledged that understanding of who Jesus is in his first epistle, when he told his readers,

". . . we have seen and testify that the Father has sent his Son to be the *Savior of the world*." [23]

Why Did Jesus Come?

When Jesus spoke to the crowd around Zacchaeus, He told them,

"The Son of Man came to *seek and save what was lost.*" [24]

Did Jesus succeed in His mission, or will the vast majority of the lost never be found?

When speaking to the crowd after His triumphal entry into Jerusalem, Jesus said,

"And I, when I am lifted up from the earth, will draw *all people* to myself." [25]

Was Jesus telling the truth when He said that, or was He exaggerating what He would actually accomplish?

The apostle Paul explained to his readers in Corinth,

"For as in Adam *all die*, so in Christ *all will be made alive.*" [26]

He told Timothy,

". . . there is one God and one mediator between God and mankind, the man Christ Jesus, *who gave himself as a ransom for all people.*" [27]

He went on to say,

33

> "This is a trustworthy saying that
> deserves full acceptance. That is why
> we labor and strive, because we have
> put our hope in the living God, who is
> the *Savior of all people*, and especially
> of those who believe." [28]

And the apostle John told his readers that Christ

> ". . . is the atoning sacrifice for our sins,
> and not only for ours but also *for the
> sins of the whole world*." [29]

Were Paul and John, like Jesus, guilty of
dramatically overstating what God would
accomplish in Christ? No!

According to the Bible, Jesus Christ is the Savior
of the world who came to redeem all mankind!

Who Is God?

The God of the Bible is good. His love is
unconditional. His power is irresistible. And He
never gives up!

That's why He didn't abandon Adam and Eve
when they sinned in the Garden of Eden. That's
why He didn't abandon Israel when its people
turned away from Him to follow other gods.

That's why He won't abandon you, or me, or any of those He created.

God's love and faithfulness were communicated over and over throughout the Old Testament when the priests and the people praised the God of heaven.

> "He is good; His love endures forever!"[30]

It's what David understood, especially after he fell far short of being the man after God's own heart in the affair with Bathsheba, the wife of Uriah. David wrote in Psalm 102,

> "He will not always accuse, nor will he harbor his anger forever; he does not treat us as our sins deserve or repay us according to our iniquities."[31]

God's good purposes for judgment are expressed clearly in the book of Lamentations.

> "For men are not cast off by the Lord forever. Though he brings grief, he will show compassion, so great is his unfailing love. For he does not

willingly bring affliction or grief to
the children of men." [32]

Similarly, the prophet Micah ends his book with
these words,

> "You do not stay angry forever but
> delight to show mercy. You will
> again have compassion on us; you
> will tread our sins underfoot and hurl
> all our iniquities into the depths of
> the sea. You will be true to Jacob,
> and show mercy to Abraham, as you
> pledged on oath to our fathers in
> days long ago." [33]

It's what the prophets proclaimed as they looked
to the distant future to see how God will treat the
nations.

> "The LORD Almighty will prepare a
> feast of rich food for *all peoples* . . .
> he will destroy the shroud that
> enfolds *all peoples*, the sheet that
> covers *all nations*; he will swallow
> up death forever. The Sovereign
> LORD will wipe away the tears from
> *all faces*." [34]

Even Sodom, a city that had experienced

punishment from which the imagery of hell was developed, isn't without hope of restoration. After telling Jerusalem that she not only walked in the ways of Sodom and Samaria, and became even more depraved than they, Ezekiel explained that God

> "will restore the fortunes of Sodom and her daughters and of Samaria and her daughters, and your fortunes along with them . . . And your sisters, Sodom with her daughters and Samaria with her daughters, will return to what they were before, and you and your daughters will return to what you were before." [35]

God's Amazing Grace

God's grace is far greater than mankind's sin. In his letter to the Christians in Rome, the apostle Paul explained that where sin increased, grace increased all the more! [36]

He went on to point out that all mankind has sinned. All mankind needs a Savior. And God will have mercy on all mankind.

> "For God has bound all men over to

disobedience so that he may have mercy on them all." [37]

Paul told his readers in Corinth,

"God was reconciling the world to himself in Christ, not counting men's sins against them." [38]

And in his letter to the Colossians, he said that just as God *created* everything and everyone in heaven and on earth through Christ, so He will *reconcile to Himself* everything and everyone in heaven and on earth through Christ.

"For in him all things were created: things in heaven and on earth, visible and invisible, whether thrones or powers or rulers or authorities; all things have been created through him and for him. . . For God was pleased to have all his fullness dwell in him, and through him to reconcile to himself all things, whether things on earth or things in heaven, by making peace through his blood, shed on the cross." [39]

The Nature and Character of God

Endless, conscious suffering in hell was not the teaching of the Early Church. It's not the teaching of the Bible. And it's also contrary to what Scripture reveals about the nature and character of God.

God *Wants* to Save All Mankind

It's not uncommon to see a bumper sticker on a car or graffiti on a wall that says, *"God loves you."* It's so common that it's almost become a cliché. But is it true? Does God really love *you?* The religious leaders of Jesus' day didn't think so. They thought God only loved people like them. So Jesus told them three parables to show them God's heart.

The Good Shepherd is not satisfied with the restoration of 99% of what is his. He seeks *until* he finds the one lost sheep. The Woman with ten silver coins wasn't satisfied to have 90% of her wealth. She searched *until* the coin that was lost was found. The Prodigal Son's Father waited *until* his lost son returned after completely messing up his life. He welcomed him joyfully, and his son was restored.

The Apostle Paul told Timothy,

> "This is good, and pleases God our Savior, who wants *all people to be saved and to come to the knowledge of the truth*." [40]

And Peter told his readers,

> "The Lord is not slow in keeping his promise, as some understand slowness. Instead, he is patient with you, *not wanting anyone to perish, but everyone to come to repentance*." [41]

God is *Able* to Save All Mankind

It's important to remember that God wants to save all mankind. But it's equally important to remember that God is *able* to save all mankind. He is the all-powerful Lord of all creation, who accomplishes everything He intends to do.

> "There is no wisdom, no insight, no plan

that can succeed against the LORD." [42]

"The LORD does whatever pleases him, in the heavens and on the earth, in the seas and all their depths." [43]

"I know that You can do all things, And that no purpose of Yours can be thwarted." [44]

"Nothing is impossible with God." [45]

In Matthew 16:18, Jesus says to Peter, "on this rock I will build my church, and the gates of *Hades* will not overcome it." Gates are defensive structures. Jesus is saying that His Church will attack and destroy the enemy's gates, bringing release to those held captive by it.

Similarly, Jesus tells the apostle John that He holds the "keys of death and Hades." [46] Jesus is certainly not the devil's doorkeeper. He does not lock the door to keep the captives inside. The gates of death and *Hades* open to Him. He is the Victor who defeats His enemies and releases the captives.

God *Will* Save All Mankind

A few years ago, I was in a polite discussion with

a theologian who believes that God wants to and is able to save everyone, but he thought God won't necessarily do so because He has given mankind a free will. This theologian felt it was necessary to leave open the possibility that some people may choose to resist God throughout eternity.

I explained that I agreed that it was theoretically possible, but that Scripture has revealed that it won't happen because God has shown us what the end will actually be.

The Apostle Paul told his readers in Philippi what will happen at the end of time.

> ". . . at the name of Jesus *every* knee will bow – in heaven and on earth and under the earth – and *every* tongue confess that Jesus Christ is Lord to the glory of God the Father." [47]

And this is not forced submission. It is freely given. Every use in the New Testament of the word translated "confess" in this passage connotes voluntary confession – *to freely, openly, wholeheartedly acknowledge or give praise.* God doesn't force praise from vanquished enemies, and He doesn't accept hypocritical or feigned praise.

The New Jerusalem

At the very end of the last book of the Bible, we learn of a glorious city that has come down from heaven, filled with beauty that is beyond description. We are told that the gates of the city are *always* open. The fruit of the tree of life is *always* available. Its leaves are for the healing of the nations. And at that time, there will no longer be any curse. Then Jesus Himself says,

> "Blessed are those who wash their robes, that they may have the right to the tree of life and may go through the gates into the city." [48]

So who are those outside the city who are invited to wash their robes and go through the gates into the city? They're the same ones who, just a few verses earlier, were said to have their place in the Lake of Fire. Like the Prodigal Son, they are living outside the blessing of their Father. Why? Because those who are ungodly and impure are not allowed to enter through any of the city's twelve gates – while they remain in that state.

But God doesn't give up on them. In the New Jerusalem, an invitation is given,

> "The Spirit and the bride say, 'Come.'
> "And let him who hears say, "Come."
> Let the one who is thirsty, come; and let the one who wishes take the free gift of the water of life." [49]

The *bride* is the body of believers throughout history who are already in the New Jerusalem. They don't need to wash their robes and eat of the tree of life because they've already done so. They're already in the city. The Spirit and the bride are calling to those in the Lake of purifying Fire outside the gates.

The Greatest News
Ever Announced!

Ultimate Restoration is based on the fact that the God of heaven – *that Being than which none greater can be conceived* – is good!

He is not *partial* – favoring some over others.

He does not *change* – acting graciously toward sinners while they're alive on earth, but then withdrawing His hand of mercy at death.

He is not *cruel* – able to save all, but choosing rather to consign most of the human race to endless, conscious suffering.

And He is not *weak* – desiring to save all, but ultimately powerless to do so.

The true teaching of the Bible is that hell is real, but it doesn't last forever. Evil will not remain a part of God's creation forever. At the end of time, all those God created in His image will enjoy the peace and joy of being in His presence. Jesus Christ *succeeded* in His mission to seek and save what was lost.

That really is the greatest news ever announced!

Heaven's Doors

A more complete development of the information presented here can be found in my book, *Heaven's Doors . . . Wider Than You Ever Believed!* which was awarded the Silver Medal in Theology in the Illumination Book Awards for exemplary Christian literature.

The book is available as a paperback, eBook or as an audiobook on Amazon.com.

Endnotes

1 Clement of Alexandria, *Stromata*, Book VII, Chapter 2
2 Clement of Alexandria, *Stromata,* Book VII, Chapter 16
3 Gregory of Nyssa, *Catechetical Oration*, VIII
4 Gregory of Nyssa, Sermon I Corinthians 15:28, *Documents in Early Christian Thought*, edited by Maurice Wiles & Mark Santer, Cambridge University Press, 1975, p. 257
5 Ilaria L.E. Ramelli, *The Christian Doctrine of Apokatastasis,* BRILL, Leiden Boston, 2013, p. 11
6 St. Augustine, *Enchiridion: On Faith, Hope and Love*, Chapter xxix, 112, translated by Albert C. Outler, 1955
7 Edward Beecher, *History of Opinions on the Scriptural Doctrine of Retribution*, D. Appleton and Company, New York, 1878, p.141
8 Jonah 2:6
9 St. Augustine, *City of God Against the Pagans*, tr. Henry Bettenson, (London:Penguin, 1972), 1001-2
10 Matthew 24:3
11 Ecclesiastes 6:3
12 Mark 3:28-29
13 Matthew 12:32
14 Luke 13:23
15 Matthew 7:13-14
16 Hebrew 6:4-6
17 Matthew 19:25-26
18 Revelation 21:8

[19] Revelation 20:10
[20] Luke 2:10-11
[21] John 1:29
[22] Luke 4:42
[23] I John 4:14
[24] Luke 19:10
[25] John 12:32
[26] I Cor. 15:22
[27] I Timothy 2:3-6
[28] I Timothy 4:9-10
[29] I John 2:2
[30] Cf. II Chronicles 7:3
[31] Psalm 103:8-14
[32] Lamentations 3:31-33
[33] Micah 7:17-20
[34] Isaiah 25:6-8.
[35] Ezekiel 16:53-55
[36] Romans 5:20
[37] Romans 11:32
[38] II Corinthians 5:19
[39] Colossians 1:16, 19-20
[40] I Timothy 2:3-4
[41] II Peter 3:9
[42] Proverbs 21:30
[43] Psalm 135:6
[44] Job 42:2
[45] Luke 1:37
[46] Revelation 1:18
[47] Philippians 2:10-11
[48] Revelation 22:14
[49] Revelation 22:17

Made in the USA
Columbia, SC
15 October 2024